Beachwood Drive

by Steven Leigh Morris

A Samuel French Acting Edition

New York Hollywood London Toronto

SAMUELFRENCH.COM

Copyright © 2009 by Steven Leigh Morris

Cover art by Abingdon Theatre Company

ALL RIGHTS RESERVED

CAUTION: Professionals and amateurs are hereby warned that *BEACHWOOD DRIVE* is subject to a royalty. It is fully protected under the copyright laws of the United States of America, the British Commonwealth, including Canada, and all other countries of the Copyright Union. All rights, including professional, amateur, motion picture, recitation, lecturing, public reading, radio broadcasting, television and the rights of translation into foreign languages are strictly reserved. In its present form the play is dedicated to the reading public only.

The amateur live stage performance rights to *BEACHWOOD DRIVE* are controlled exclusively by Samuel French, Inc., and royalty arrangements and licenses must be secured well in advance of presentation. PLEASE NOTE that amateur royalty fees are set upon application in accordance with your producing circumstances. When applying for a royalty quotation and license please give us the number of performances intended, dates of production, your seating capacity and admission fee. Royalties are payable one week before the opening performance of the play to Samuel French, Inc., at 45 W. 25th Street, New York, NY 10010.

Royalty of the required amount must be paid whether the play is presented for charity or gain and whether or not admission is charged.

Stock royalty quoted upon application to Samuel French, Inc.

For all other rights than those stipulated above, apply to Samuel French, Inc., at 45 W. 25th Street, New York, NY 10010.

Particular emphasis is laid on the question of amateur or professional readings, permission and terms for which must be secured in writing from Samuel French, Inc.

Copying from this book in whole or in part is strictly forbidden by law, and the right of performance is not transferable.

Whenever the play is produced the following notice must appear on all programs, printing and advertising for the play: "Produced by special arrangement with Samuel French, Inc."

Due authorship credit must be given on all programs, printing and advertising for the play.

ISBN 978-0-573-69606-0   Printed in U.S.A.   #29003

No one shall commit or authorize any act or omission by which the copyright of, or the right to copyright, this play may be impaired.

No one shall make any changes in this play for the purpose of production.

Publication of this play does not imply availability for performance. Both amateurs and professionals considering a production are strongly advised in their own interests to apply to Samuel French, Inc., for written permission before starting rehearsals, advertising, or booking a theatre.

No part of this book may be reproduced, stored in a retrieval system, or transmitted in any form, by any means, now known or yet to be invented, including mechanical, electronic, photocopying, recording, videotaping, or otherwise, without the prior written permission of the publisher.

IMPORTANT BILLING AND CREDIT REQUIREMENTS

All producers of *BEACHWOOD DRIVE* must give credit to the Author of the Play in all programs distributed in connection with performances of the Play, and in all instances in which the title of the Play appears for the purposes of advertising, publicizing or otherwise exploiting the Play and/or a production. The name of the Author *must* appear on a separate line on which no other name appears, immediately following the title and *must* appear in size of type not less than fifty percent of the size of the title type.

ABINGDON THEATRE COMPANY
Jan Buttram *Artistic Director*
Samuel J. Bellinger *Managing Director*

Presents

beachwood drive

by Steven Leigh Morris
directed by Alan Mandell

Cast
(in order of appearance)

Nadya	Lena Starostina
Hansonia	Brenda Thomas
Katerina	Kat Peters
Rocky	David Medina
Vera	Maria Silverman
William Cromwell	Peter Brouwer

The action takes place in Los Angeles. The recent past.

Beachwood Drive will be performed with a ten-minute intermission.

Abingdon Theatre Company dedicates the 2008-2009 season of new American plays to the memory of George Grizzard and Madeline Gilford.

Set Design Ken Larson *Costume Design* Deborah J. Caney *Lighting Design* Matthew McCarthy
Sound Design David Margolin Lawson *Video Design* Kymberly Mortensen
Production Manager Ian Grunes D+P *Production Stage Manager* Genevieve Ortiz
Casting Director William Schill *Associate Artistic Director* Kim T. Sharp
Press Representative Shirley Herz Associates

Beachwood Drive was developed in Los Angeles by Playwrights Arena (Jon Lawrence Rivera, Artistic Director) and in New York by Abingdon Theatre Company.
The play is dedicated to Cathy Carlton and Alan Mandell.

October 17 - November 16, 2008

JUNE HAVOC THEATRE
Abingdon Theatre Arts Complex
312 West 36th Street, 1st Floor, New York City
www.abingdontheatre.org

Beachwood Drive is made possible with the generous support of Z. Clark Branson.

Abingdon Theatre Company's 2008-2009 season is supported, in part, by public funds from the New York State Council on the Arts and the New York City Department of Cultural Affairs.

Dedicated to Developing and Producing New American Theatre

CHARACTERS

HANSONIA - 40s, African-American female novelist and arts writer for a Los Angeles-based alternative newspaper

NADYA - 30s, female immigrant from Odessa, Ukraine, now a prostitute in Los Angeles

ROCKY - Mid 30s male, Latino meat packer from El Monte, California; descended from Tongva branch of the Gabrielino Indians, the indigenous tribe that dominated the Los Angeles area prior to the incursions of the Spanish in the mid 1700s.

VERA - 40s, female immigrant from Moscow, runs an escort service in Los Angeles

WILLIAM CROMWELL - 60s, a fatigued Caucasian homicide investigator for the Los Angeles Police Department; has tried in vain numerous times to retire

KATERINA - Nadya's 10 year-old daughter

SETTING

The action is set in the present, in various locales, including 1) an apartment on Beachwood Drive: a semi-artsy, semi-upscale district of actors and Industry execs that winds up towards the Hollywood Sign, 2) a cottage bungalow, next door to the apartment on Beachwood Drive, 3) an interview room at the Hollywood Station of the Los Angeles Police Department. Each setting need only be distinguished by a suggestion – e.g. a wall hanging, a piece of furniture or a shift in the placement thereof – rather than encumbering details, as the play's structure is somewhat dreamlike.

PROLOGUE

(We hear the bucolic piano of Schumann's "Of Strange Lands and People" from his "Kindersehnen" as we see on a screen the projected image from a computer. It slowly becomes recognizable as a pornography web site: a "video stream" picture of a Caucasian woman, wearing a halter top and panties, rollicking on a bed and smiling into the web cam. The motion, rather than being cinematically seamless, is jumpy. Rather than a live video with its transmission of fluid motion, the web cam image is a series of static poses that change every five seconds or so, grainy pictures of the model smiling coyly, running her fingers through her hair. Adjusting the strap of a halter top to reveal a sliver of breast before pulling the strap back up. Soon, the camera angle reveals a computer keyboard in the bed with the model. She pulls it within her reach and types diligently.)

(In a corner of the screen, we see a "dialogue box" with the following, running text:)

<Jimmy:> Sometimes, at places, like intersections, at red lights, I see you.

<Betty:> Oh, at red lights. That's rich.

<Jimmy:> No, I mean, you know what I mean.

<Betty:> Sure, I know what you mean.

<Jimmy:> I mean on hazy afternoons, out by Lincoln Park, by the lake, by the fountain, I'll be waiting at a light, and that's when you come to me, out of the mist, like a dream, like an angel.

<Betty:> Oh, stop.

<Jimmy:> Don't tell me to stop. You've never seen me. I see you everywhere, but you've never seen me.

<Betty:> From your words. I see you through your words.

<Jimmy:> How can we meet?

(Suddenly, the picture of "Betty" squelches and disappears into static as the music fades.)

ACT 1
("HANSONIA")

(Lights up on **HANSONIA**'s *bungalow on Beachwood Drive: a hardwood floor, an upholstered chair, a throw rug, a wooden desk and bookstand, both overflowing with papers and books, a suspended African mask and suspended tribal-themed paintings. No discernible walls, or door.)*

*(***HANSONIA**, *an African-American woman in her 40s, stands awkwardly leaning over her desk.)*

(In the upholstered chair sits **NADYA**, *a Caucasian woman, mid-30s, recognizable as "Betty" from the webcam transmission seen in the prologue.)*

*(***HANSONIA** *and* **NADYA**'s *dialogue overlaps:)*

HANSONIA. The point being, well, the point *not* being the money…

NADYA. I can pay.

HANSONIA. Of course.

NADYA. I *will* pay…

HANSONIA. It's really not necessary. We're next door neighbors.

NADYA. What difference does *that* make? It's your time. I should pay you.

HANSONIA. It's *baby-sitting* for heaven's sake.

NADYA. I *must*…I must pay.

(pause)

HANSONIA. Okay. Whatever. Tea, you said?

NADYA. Please.

HANSONIA. That'll be two dollars, plus tip.

NADYA. Very funny.

HANSONIA. I use leaves, not bags. Never use bags.

NADYA. Yes, yes, me too. Exactly. The brew. It just isn't the same.

HANSONIA. The leaves are from Bombay, not Russia. I hope that's all right.

NADYA. Hansonia, I'm not Russian.

HANSONIA. Sorry. Is there even such a thing as Ukrainian tea?

NADYA. Everything grows in Ukraine.

HANSONIA. Nadya, to me, Odessa is still Russia. Gorbachev is still in power, I'm nostalgic that way. He was your Lincoln. Wanted to preserve the union. Yeltsin was Robert E. Lee. Ended up selling the farm. I remember what used to be called the *balance* of power.

NADYA. Hansonia, please, I'm not political. I hate politics.

(pause)

HANSONIA. I still think Gorbachev had the right idea.

NADYA. Well, good for him.

HANSONIA. *(playing a slightly cruel game, but with humor)* And now the Western wolf is unfettered, dancing the privatization jig like a Banshee. Even Putin's crackdowns, that's just window dressing…

NADYA. *(tensely)* The walls have ears! *(almost whispering)* I am not yet an American citizen, and I would like to be.

*(Pause, **NADYA**'s paranoia is a revelation for **HANSONIA**, who exits. **NADYA** rises, stares at the suspended African mask. **HANSONIA** reenters with a tea service, a Russian samovar and two cups. Seeing the samovar, **NADYA** smiles.)*

HANSONIA. *(referring to the samovar)* St. Petersburg, 1992. Cultural exchange, Russian and American novelists. The Russians wound up in Houston, in August, poor bastards.

(HANSONIA sets the service on her desk. Pours two cups of tea, offers NADYA one of them. NADYA remains standing.)

I didn't mean to make you uncomfortable. I just forgot where you come from.

NADYA. *(remains standing)* I know you're a kind person. I wouldn't be here if you weren't. *(referring to the mask)* Where did you get this?

HANSONIA. Kampala. Literary conference, 1998. It's a Baganda mask. The tribe dates back to the 14th century. You wouldn't know it to see Uganda today…

NADYA. You keep bringing the world to your home.

HANSONIA. Pieces of it. It's sort of my job.

NADYA. It's a beautiful home.

HANSONIA. It's kind of dusty and…

NADYA. The character.

HANSONIA. Thank you.

NADYA. There aren't many people I would trust with my daughter.

HANSONIA. Yes, I believe you; I'm quite honored, actually. How old is she, exactly.

NADYA. When we met, by the bus bench, I felt you were somebody I could trust. I almost never get that feeling from…from anybody. She's ten.

HANSONIA. Nadya, we only met yesterday. I said hello, you said hello back, and then we were talking about Chagal. How many people on the street can one engage in a conversation about Chagal?

NADYA. If you could come at six, we could all spend some time together. So Katerina can feel more comfortable with you. I know she likes you already. I'll leave by seven. The code is 502.

HANSONIA. This is only the second time we've met. Are you always so trusting – I mean, with your own daughter?

NADYA. *(after a brief pause)* Are you judging me?

HANSONIA. No!

NADYA. There's a situation I have to deal with. Tonight. A friend is dying. In the hospital. I found out about it yesterday. You seem like someone I can trust.

(silence)

HANSONIA. Is there anything I should bring?

NADYA. Maybe some of your art books. That would be good for her.

HANSONIA. I'm not…I'm not experienced with children. I have none of my own.

NADYA. I know.

HANSONIA. How?

NADYA. I can tell, from your home.

HANSONIA. *(almost defensive)* I have several nieces and nephews.

NADYA. Then what are you worried about?

HANSONIA. Yes…

(pause)

NADYA. So we'll see you tomorrow at six.

HANSONIA. Right.

*(**NADYA** sets her cup on the desk and crosses upstage into darkness. The lights abruptly shift to an overhead shaft, like a broad circular spotlight, on **HANSONIA**. Her words are now in the direction of the audience, who is a jury, or a detective.)*

"A friend is dying," she said. "In the hospital." Of course I knew she was lying. But why was she trusting me, almost a stranger, with her daughter?

So I'm babysitting Cathy – Katerina, her mother called her. Cathy and I are watching TV, which I never do at home. But I'm not in my bungalow, with my cats and dust and re-heated coffee. No. I'm in the gleaming condo next door, on the fourth floor, in a building with a buzzer and palm trees that smack against the windows in the Santa Ana winds. Eleven p.m. Cathy and me sitting on the rug playing Nintendo. The coffee-table book of glossy Kandinsky graphics that

I brought, especially for this occasion, remains unopened. Nadya's still not home. The game gives me nightmares, I say. The violence. Cathy calls me a wimp and turns off the TV. We both stare at the cream condo walls. I sense a ghost behind the window and curl my fingers into the carpet shag – next to the Styrofoam box with the cold Chinese food. Bare walls. Not a trace of Old World decor. No embroidered curtains, no hand-painted plates on the walls. Spotless, like a clinic.

*(Through the following, **KATERINA**, a 10 year-old girl in overalls and sneakers, creeps into the periphery of light, like a ghost. The spot opens into a general wash.)*

HANSONIA. How old were you when you left Odessa?

KATERINA. Eight.

HANSONIA. Do you remember it?

KATERINA. Some

HANSONIA. And what do you remember?

(She shrugs.)

HANSONIA. Do you miss it?

KATERINA. No.

HANSONIA. Were you rich or poor?

(She shrugs.)

HANSONIA. Did you ever go hungry?

KATERINA. No.

HANSONIA. So tell me something about Odessa.

KATERINA. Grandma and grandpa…

*(**KATERINA** falls silent. Stoic.)*

HANSONIA. And how is it different from Los Angeles?

KATERINA. Mama has many more boyfriends here. *(brief pause)* Mama says one day we'll live someplace else.

HANSONIA. Like where?

KATERINA. I don't know.

HANSONIA. Odessa?

KATERINA. Oh no. We couldn't go back there.

HANSONIA. Why not?

KATERINA. Vera.

HANSONIA. Who's Vera?

KATERINA. Mama's boss.

HANSONIA. So why can't your mom just move? Get another job?

KATERINA. Vera's mean.

HANSONIA. Mean?

KATERINA. We tried to move but Vera wouldn't let us.

HANSONIA. Move where?

KATERINA. Chicago. Mama's got a cousin there.

HANSONIA. How could Vera stop you?

KATERINA. It's not Vera. It's her men!

(*A woman crosses behind the window in shadows.* **HANSONIA** *turns suddenly.*)

Why are you always so scared?

HANSONIA. Ghosts…I still believe in ghosts.

(*Through the following,* **KATERINA** *slowly withdraws into the darkness. Spotlight on* **HANSONIA**.)

HANSONIA. (*in the direction of the audience, which is a jury, or a detective*) She came to see me two times, in my home. I work mostly from home, even for the newspaper I write for, they let me, they *encourage* me to work at home, probably because of my depression. Morbid depression. Clinical depression. I refused their medicines because I *welcome* my illness, though of course I don't enjoy it. It challenges me and fuels my creativity, leads to clairvoyance. I learned this from reading about Abraham Lincoln, who repaired a fractured nation while similarly depressed. He'd walk into a party and read poems about the pointlessness of life and the inevitability of death, yes, at dinner parties! And in such a frame of mind, he repaired this fractured nation. And that's why I refuse their medicines. I live by two edicts: Never take antidepressants and never watch television.

I want to write an American story told by a white member of a Southern lynch mob. That was actually James Baldwin's idea, and I'd like to take him up on it. Pick up where Mark Twain and William Faulkner left off. We have to understand the violence from the victimizers' view as well as the victims', then the story speaks to *everybody*, speaks to our actions from Manila to Mississippi, to Baghdad. I'm sorry – what was your question?

What did I know at the time? Empirically, nothing. But I felt for that child and the danger she floated in. Though I fear that's of little use for finding the people you're after.

(Pause. Through the following, **KATERINA** *wanders back into the periphery of the light.)*

(Lights shift into a general wash.)

HANSONIA. Are you okay? Are you locked out?

KATERINA. Mama's got visitors.

HANSONIA. Uh huh. You want a glass of milk?

KATERINA. No.

HANSONIA. Are you hungry?

KATERINA. No.

HANSONIA. Does she know where you are?

KATERINA. Who?

HANSONIA. Your mother.

KATERINA. She told me to come here.

HANSONIA. A phone call might have been considerate.

KATERINA. She wanted to, but Vera was in the room. *(seeing* **HANSONIA**'s *perplexed expression)* Are you married?

HANSONIA. Men find me depressing. Women too.

KATERINA. Where'd you get all these paintings?

HANSONIA. They're my father's. He was a collector. He left them to me.

KATERINA. Is this why you're always so spooked?

HANSONIA. I am *not* always spooked!

KATERINA. What's in the box?

HANSONIA. Mementos. A ring from my Aunt Mattie. A tie clip my cousin George used to wear. Help yourself.

(**KATERINA** *reaches into the box and pulls out a miniature oil painting, no frame, peeling and crusted.*)

KATERINA. What's this?

HANSONIA. A portrait. Don't know how it got there. She's a woman who now comes to me in my dreams. She pays me visits, just like you. She says my blood is hers. Came from the Ivory Coast, she says, to the Charleston Bay. 1619. Locked in steerage. Bodies stacked five high. Coated in vomit. Visited by rats. Lost five children and a husband on the passage. Almost died herself. She says I must write her story.

KATERINA. Will you?

HANSONIA. No...I don't like being told what to do. So she comes to me in my dreams and gives me nightmares, out of spite.

(**KATERINA** *just stares at her. Feeling the awkwardness,* **KATERINA** *returns the portrait to the memento box and picks up a newspaper she recognizes.*)

That's the paper I write for.

(**KATERINA** *flips through it, shows* **HANSONIA** *an advertisement near the back.*)

KATERINA. There's mama's picture.

HANSONIA. *(observing, shocked)* "Russian beauties. www.exoticbeauties.com" *(pause)* Do you know what "adult services" means?

(**KATERINA** *shakes her head, "no."*)

Good. Do you know why her photo is in the paper?

KATERINA. Because she's beautiful.

HANSONIA. Yes...Exactly. Let me make you a sandwich.

KATERINA. No thanks.

HANSONIA. *(slightly irritated)* Do you not eat? Do you not drink? *(gathering composure)* Do you have friends to play with after school?

KATERINA. No.

HANSONIA. Too enigmatic?

KATERINA. Huh?

HANSONIA. They don't understand you.

KATERINA. I don't know.

(She stares at the painting.)

HANSONIA. You're always welcome here. I also had an absent mother. I was also lost in the world at your age.

(HANSONIA** approaches **KATERINA** and slips a lock of the child's hair through her fingers.* **KATERINA** *slips back into darkness. Spotlight on* **HANSONIA, to audience, or jury, or detective)*

HANSONIA. So in her office, I ask Charlotte – she's the editor – if there's nothing we can do about the ads in the back of the newspaper. She stares at me as though I've lost my mind.

"I find the ads personally offensive – repugnant," I say.

"Me too," she replies. "But that's all beside the point. Which is a free market."

"On the Web," I say, "MSNBC is in partnership with the *Washington Post* and *Newsweek,* leaving it to compete, if that's the correct term, with only *two* companies that can match its technological prowess: Time-Warner and Disney. Keep in mind that Time-Warner owns CNN while Disney controls ABC and ESPN. So where's the free market?"

"In the back of our newspaper," she says.

(After a pause, **KATERINA** *enters the periphery of light, holding a binder.)*

Dusk. I'm staring at a blank computer screen. Two weeks since Cathy's last visit. You know the next part. I gaze upwards, across the room, and there she is.

KATERINA. *(ebullient)* I have something to show you. It took me a week.

(Lights shift into a general wash.)

HANSONIA. *(to* **KATERINA***)* How are you? What have you been doing?

KATERINA. This.

(She opens the binder, removing a series of sheets, a tender ritual, the unveiling of butcher paper cut into small pieces – crayon drawings. **KATERINA** *lays them on the floor.)*

You're the first person I've shown. It's crayon.

HANSONIA. Is that an apartment building?

KATERINA. Uh huh.

HANSONIA. Soviet style. Odessa?

KATERINA. It's grandma…And grandpa.

HANSONIA. *(shocked by the contents)* They're still there?

KATERINA. Uh huh.

HANSONIA. And what do they do?

KATERINA. Nothing.

HANSONIA. Do you ever speak with them?

KATERINA. Sometimes

HANSONIA. On the phone?

KATERINA. Uh huh.

HANSONIA. And what do they say?

KATERINA. That I should go home.

HANSONIA. To Odessa?

KATERINA. Uh huh.

HANSONIA. Do they talk about their parents?

KATERINA. Their parents are dead. They were shot. In a ditch. With their friends.

HANSONIA. But do they talk about them?

KATERINA. They tell stories.

HANSONIA. And do you remember these stories?

KATERINA. Some. Not really.

HANSONIA. Next time you speak with them, ask them to tell you more stories. Then you must remember them. It's very important. Will you do that? For me?

KATERINA. Okay.

(**HANSONIA** *returns the papers to* **KATERINA**, *who spontaneously holds her, clutching the child, who returns the affection before slipping away into darkness, as the lighting closes in on an wide spotlight pool.*)

HANSONIA. *(to audience, or jury, or detective)* Those drawings…were *horrific* – image after image of figures lying in blood, shot in a bathtub, strangled, hanging from a doorway, and that's when I fully absorbed the reality of the danger.
When Nadya was released the following morning, I was already back here.

(**NADYA** *bursts in, numb with despair.*)

NADYA. Never. Not in my life.

HANSONIA. Never what?

NADYA. You will *never* see her again. Not in this house.

HANSONIA. What are you talking about?

NADYA. My daughter. Or me.

HANSONIA. Okay. And why is that?

NADYA. Like you need to ask.

HANSONIA. Well, yes, I do.

NADYA. I spent the night in *jail*! Does that mean anything to you!?

HANSONIA. It was *me* you called, to take care of Cathy, to bail you out, remember?

NADYA. Who else *was* there?

HANSONIA. So what's the problem?

NADYA. Someone reported me.

HANSONIA. It wasn't *me*.

NADYA. Oh, please…

HANSONIA. What makes you think it was *me*? It could have been any neighbor. Talk about traffic. They might as well have built an off-ramp from the Hollywood Freeway leading right up to your door!

NADYA. It was a sting operation. Somebody *told* them.

HANSONIA. For heaven's sake, they could've been tipped off from the *newspaper*. You *advertise*, remember! You're on the *Web*! You're not that difficult to *find*!

(*Pause, as* **NADYA** *paces back and forth before spinning in on* **HANSONIA**.)

NADYA. You're lying.

HANSONIA. (*after a slight pause*) I'm not lying. I did tell a friend about your situation, that you were a *victim*.

NADYA. What friend?

HANSONIA. He job is to protect victims.

NADYA. Fuck!...Fuck! I've *never* trusted you.

HANSONIA. You're distraught.

NADYA. I don't trust anyone in this fucking city of smiles and hugs. Where I come from, people on the streets are like ice, which is exactly how they feel. No, "Hi, how-ya-*doo*oin — good-to-*see*e *e*-you-again" bullshit before they cut your throat.

HANSONIA. Nobody cut your throat.

NADYA. *Somebody* did. What business did you have talking to *anybody* about me...

HANSONIA. What kind of mother leaves her daughter with a stranger while she's out turning tricks?!

NADYA. You keep my daughter out of this! Don't you even *speak* about my daughter! You understand *nothing*! Do you understand *that*, at least?

HANSONIA. All right then. (**NADYA** *turns away.*) Look at me, damn you, Look at me!

(**NADYA** *faces her.*)

I did *not* report you. I was trying to *help* you...*and* Katerina.

(**NADYA** *turns away.*)

I am your friend. Your *only* friend, it seems. (*pause*) How did you get caught?

NADYA. I told you it was a *sting*...

HANSONIA. The guy comes in...Don't you *screen* these people?

NADYA. He asked me how much I charged and for what.

HANSONIA. And you told him.

NADYA. Yes. Next thing I was in handcuffs. Thank goodness Katerina was in school.

HANSONIA. Don't they train you people for situations like that?

NADYA. Just like that. Ten words, and I'm in jail.

HANSONIA. Aren't you supposed to wait until they're completely undressed? 'Cause a cop will never completely undress.

NADYA. Yes, I knew that.

HANSONIA. So what were you *thinking*?

NADYA. Obviously, I *wasn't thinking*.

(silence)

HANSONIA. What did you come here for? Other than to berate me.

NADYA. To say good-bye.

HANSONIA. What for? *(pause, distraught)* What for!!?

NADYA. It was stupid. Everything I've done this week has been stupid. I'm sorry I troubled you.

*(The lights shift into wide spotlight on **HANSONIA**.)*

HANSONIA. *(to audience)* And Katerina never came to visit again. I think that's what hurt me the most. Sometimes, I still see her on the bus bench, a ghost behind a blur of traffic. Or maybe it's really her. Staring aimless up Beachwood Drive, squinting into the sun.

*(A tight circle of white light, beams down from overhead on **ROCKY**, a Latino man in his 30s, dressed in a tan, net tank top that reveals Native American tattoos [feathers and headdresses] on his muscular arms and shoulders, black sport trousers, and sneakers. He has flowing shoulder-length black hair that he tosses out of his face as he performs solo the Gabrielino "Bear Dance.")*

*(At **ROCKY**'s feet, a tray of incense sends a trail of smoke and scent wafting up and around him.)*

(He is positioned on the balls of his feet, knees bent, leaning slightly forward, The dance consists of him shifting his weight from one foot to the other, back and forth to the pulse of a chant that he sings. As he shifts his weight back and forth, he slowly turns in place. He holds a rattle in one hand that he shakes to help sound the dance's steady pulse, accompanied by the following chant, which he sings:)

ROCKY. Hyang ya cron-na lod-a nory
Hyang ya cron-na lod-a nory
Hyang ya cron-na lod-a nory

GGGGGRRRRRRUUUUGGGH *(with the shaking of the rattle)*
GGGGGRRRRRRUUUUGGGH

Hyang ya cron-na lod-a nory
Hyang ya cron-na lod-a nory
Hyang ya cron-na lod-a nory

(A female figure slowly crosses the stage in shadow once more, this time watching, menacing.)

ACT 2
("ROCKY")

(Lights up on a bed, a chair. Spartan design. A room in **NADYA***'s apartment. Dressed in a nightrobe,* **NADYA** *sits in the chair smoking, talking into a cellphone..)*

NADYA. *(into phone, in Russian)* Da…Da. Fsyo narmalna. Uh uh. Nee znayoo. Da. Adeen chas. Katya s-tboi? Ha-ra-shó. Uh hmm. Paka.

*(***ROCKY** *enters the playing area.* **NADYA** *hangs up, stares at* **ROCKY***. Says nothing.)*

ROCKY. What was that about?

NADYA. My daughter.

ROCKY. You have a daughter?

NADYA. That's what I just said.

*(***NADYA** *takes a long drag on her cigarette.)*

How's the tea?

ROCKY. Excellent. Fuck I don't know. I don't drink tea. I don't *like* tea.

NADYA. So why'd you ask for it?

ROCKY. Because you *offered* it. Where's yours?

NADYA. I didn't want any.

ROCKY. You have a beer?

*(***NADYA** *rises, taking* **ROCKY***'s mug before crossing out into the shadows, as* **ROCKY** *shifts to another side of the room, terribly uncomfortable.* **NADYA** *returns with a bottle of Anchor Steam, hands it to* **ROCKY** *before returning to her chair. Pause.* **NADYA** *puffs on a cigarette.)*

ROCKY. How old is she? Your daughter.

NADYA. Too young for you.

ROCKY. That's not why I'm asking.

NADYA. Good.

ROCKY. Look I'm trying to be a little bit human here, okay…Maybe you can return the ball?

NADYA. I was joking.

ROCKY. You were not joking.

NADYA. I was joking. Will you relax. She's ten.

ROCKY. Does she know what you do?

NADYA. Much of the time.

ROCKY. How you make your living?

NADYA. I don't really know. Truth is, we've never discussed it. Like I said, she's ten.

ROCKY. That is so…I'm sorry.

NADYA. What for?

ROCKY. For finding this all so disturbing.

NADYA. I'm sorry you're disturbed. How's the beer?

ROCKY. I haven't tasted it yet.

NADYA. I know. That's why I asked. Why don't you drink it and give me a break from your judgments.

ROCKY. Look, I didn't mean to…

NADYA. I know you didn't. You think I would do this if I had a choice?

ROCKY. But you *do* have a choice.

NADYA. Thanks for that information. Please drink you beer, and let's get on with this.

ROCKY. Maybe I should leave.

NADYA. If you want.

ROCKY. I don't even know your name.

NADYA. They didn't give it to you?

ROCKY. Yeah, they did. But I forgot. Natalya?

NADYA. Nadya. From the Russian verb "Nadyéyatsya" – which means to hope. Where I come from, we call that irony.

ROCKY. And all this time, I thought your name was Betty.

(**NADYA** *stares away, taking a drag from her cigarette.*)

ROCKY. So is it Betty or Nadya?

NADYA. What difference?

ROCKY. I have a right to know your name. I have an investment…You don't look much like a Betty. Betty Rubble. Betty Crocker. Nope, not you.

NADYA. I don't know those people. Who are they?

ROCKY. *(playing with the sound of her name)* Naah-dya. Is that made up too?

NADYA. How did you know about Betty? From my Web page? Of course, that's how you got the number.

ROCKY. So why didn't he say it was Betty? That operator. That's what I don't understand. I got the number from *Betty's* web site. Suddenly I'm speaking to some guy with a thick Russian accent, thicker than yours. I ask for Betty. He says they have no Betty. Two brunettes, Nina and Olga, and a dirty blonde named Nadya.

NADYA. Dirty blonde?

ROCKY. His words, not mine – it's not an insult. So I know what you look like from the web cam, even though your hair color's next to impossible to figure out, but I say, yeah, she might be a blonde, why not? And when I walk in your door, I understand I've struck gold. I found you! I've been downloading you for months, see, we've been talking to each other over the keyboard. I'm Jimmy, see. I'm the guy who dreams you up at red lights in Lincoln Park. Remember me now? *(pause)* So how's it going?

(She stares at him, as he offers his hand; she cautiously shakes it.)

You're way better looking in person.

*(**NADYA** slips off her robe and tumbles into the bed.)*

NADYA. You can leave your money on the table.

ROCKY. No problem.

*(**ROCKY** sets a wad of bills on the table.)*

NADYA. There's a shower down the hall.

*(The lights jolt into a tight circle, bearing down on **ROCKY**, speaking directly to audience, or jury or a detective.)*

ROCKY. The sides of beef are shipped in cold storage from the Central Valley. Same with the pork, the lamb. Mutton. Poultry we don't deal with. That's another division. And my job is to stand at a steel table and slice 'em into sirloins and rump roasts and tenderloins and pork chops and lamb chops and…Ten hours a day more or less. Seven years give or take. Wearing a bloodied apron, brushing away the flies. Buzz saw and hatchet slicing and chopping through bone and fat, little specks of blood flying like sparks. Flying right into my face sometimes. S'posed to wear gloves, but I don't. 'Cause I like the *feel* of the stuff, the raw animal muscle. I like the sound of the *slap* when I flip it over, onto the conveyer belt. This is music to a butcher, this is the pulse…

July 11, that was the first night we actually met. Betty and me. Nadya was her real name, from Odessa, so she said. That was the first time in 25 years of marriage I'd been unfaithful. *(brief pause)* Second time, actually, if you call if you call it unfaithful to French kiss a temp secretary outside a meat-packing plant. And the first time, what was remarkable to me, after an hour, I paid for an hour, $200 including tip, after an hour, she called on the phone and said something. And I wasn't dressed or nothing. After she hung up, she said we could go another hour, it was fine with her. She wasn't supposed to, but she just told them I paid for *another* hour, which I didn't, and I thought that was remarkable, that maybe this was something more than just another…sale.

About a years back, we got a computer for Tony, that's my son. For his 14th birthday. Not much of an athlete or a scholar, my boy. Got a "B minus" in Spanish, and that's pretty humiliating when your last name's Gonzales, and your Salvadoran grandmother speaks nothing but Spanish in the house. Video games and computers, those are his interests. Hobbies from school, from friends. Tony was the one who taught me the difference between software and hardware, it was all like Martian to me, but to him it was as basic as breathing. And sometimes you just sense the importance of something, like an instinct. So Angelica and me, we talked it over, Angelica's my wife, a deeply religious woman, goes to Church almost daily. Catholic turned Pentecostal, God save us, deeply conservative in too many ways, but even she had the wisdom to see that high tech for our son would be an investment. A desktop Toshiba with America on Line. Tony taught me how to use it. How to log on with my own password, my own I.D. But I knew *his*, see. One night, they're both asleep, I push the history button, to see what Tony had logged onto the day before. For no reason, really.

That's when this porno comes up. Yeah, it was a shock, not just the porno, but to understand that your teenage son is downloading this shit into your living room. I was even more pissed off that I couldn't block the flow. These windows are popping up on the screen like fireworks, four sometimes five at a time: Triple-X shit, from Taiwan and Poland, Australia and Argentina.

Bondage and cocksucking, men with boys, girls with dildos and donkeys, and I think *shit. (brief pause)* My son. The fruit of my loins. His tattoos I can tolerate, the piercings, fine, his gang friends I don't like but I understand – but *this*? If I don't calm down, I say to myself, I'm gonna strangle him right now, while he sleeps. So I turn off the computer, take a couple of shots of tequila and try to sleep next to my wife, who is curled up in a ball, her back to the center of the bed.

Next morning, Angelica's getting up to go to the office. She works as a clerk at the County court, I say nothing about what I saw, 'cause I know it'll give her a heart attack. But before Tony heads out to school, I say "Tony. Wait a second. Come here. Listen. No porno in this house, got it? It's still my house. And I don't want that shit in my house, so I'm having that porno blocking thing put it, soon as I can get someone to show me how to do it…You know how to do it?"

He says "no."

I say "Fine, asshole. I'll figure it out myself."

On my lunchbreak, I call AOL, they explain how to activate the parental controls, which I do that night. So now there's this strain between me and Tony. Even more than before. But I understand his curiosity, I really do. 'Cause sometimes at 2 a.m., when I couldn't sleep, I'd log on, but not to porno. There's these Web sites, you pay a monthly fee, where you can talk to people. And that's how I met "Betty," she called herself. And at first I was real slow, plunking out each letter 'cause I don't type. But when there's a need, you get quicker. And I was saying things I had never said to Angelica, would never say, and thought to myself, whooah, what is going on here?

And I tried to reconnect with Angelica. To talk to her in the same way, sexy provocative, in Spanish, in English. She just laughed. I bought her new clothes and underwear. We made love every night for a week and for a while Angelica was like a flower slowly opening, reopening. Until the guilt set in. Or maybe it was just exhaustion.

And that's when the old patterns came back: her coming home from her prayer meetings, and crawling up into a ball, with her back facing the center of the bed.

I tried to take Tony to the dance rehearsals of the Gabrielenos. I'm fifty percent Gabrieleno, And I tried to get Tony to come with me, but he was too angry… So late at night, two, three times a week, I'd log on to Betty. And we'd flirt until the sun come up…So what's going on? I mean, do you have any leads? What can I do to help, I mean, what can I do?

*(As the lights expand into a general wash, **NADYA** emerges from the periphery, wrapped in a robe. **ROCKY** takes a slug from his beer.)*

ROCKY. Sorry I'm late.

*(She motions for him to sit in the chair, which he does. **NADYA** settles onto the edge of the bed.)*

NADYA. *(lighting a cigarette)* How've you been?

ROCKY. Okay.

NADYA. Working?

ROCKY. Of course. What else?

NADYA. In the supermarket?

ROCKY. Yeah.

NADYA. Stocking shelves. *(brief pause)* I just don't understand.

ROCKY. What don't you understand?

NADYA. How a guy like you doesn't have a wife. Or a girlfriend.

ROCKY. Yeah, well it's probably the money. I don't make that much.

NADYA. But you spend it on me.

ROCKY. That's right.

NADYA. Not every woman thinks just about money.

ROCKY. That's very weird, coming from you.

NADYA. That's because you don't know me at all.

ROCKY. We've made love six times. I know you a little.

NADYA. All right. Then where do I come from?

ROCKY. Odessa.

NADYA. Good! And what did I do there?

ROCKY. I don't have a clue.

NADYA. You said you knew me?

ROCKY. You were an engineer.

NADYA. A bartender.

ROCKY. *(holding up his beer)* To you. *(**ROCKY** drinks. Pause)* And where's *your* boyfriend?

NADYA. Men aren't interested in women like me.

ROCKY. Fascinated, but not interested.

NADYA. Whatever.

ROCKY. *I* am.

*(After a brief pause, **NADYA** crosses to **ROCKY** and holds him close. After they separate, she takes a drag of her cigarette)*

ROCKY. Can we meet sometime? Outside of this room?

*(Pause, **NADYA** exhales.)*

NADYA. I think I'd like that.

ROCKY. Where's Cathy?

NADYA. With a neighbor.

ROCKY. The black woman?

NADYA. Yes, Hansonia. We have an hour. If you want.

ROCKY. If I want?

NADYA. Who are you, Jimmy?

ROCKY. Who am I?

NADYA. Where do you come from? Jimmy – Is that really your name?

ROCKY. Los Angeles.

NADYA. No, I mean like your great, great grandparents.

ROCKY. Los Angeles. We're from a very…ancient…tribe. Lived right here, on acorns and lizards and fish. For a thousand years. Built boats, weaved baskets and made jewelry. Wore tattoos, bathed every day, and laid out in saunas we built along the rivers.

NADYA. You make it sound like a dream.

ROCKY. It was just life, I guess. Until the Spanish.

NADYA. We had the Germans.

ROCKY. It's an old story. Yet here we are…making love. There's something to be said for that.

*(Suddenly, **NADYA** rises from the bed and exits the stage, causing **ROCKY** to rise, awkwardly, cross to the bed and fluff one of the pillows, for no particular reason.)*

(**NADYA** *reenters with a sketch pad in her hand, she lays it open on the bed.*)

These are yours?

NADYA. I've been doing these all my life. Now Cathy does the same. Yes, these are mine.

ROCKY. (*flipping through the pages*) They're just shapes and colors.

NADYA. Emotions, that's all. There's no story there. This one I did when I was 15.

ROCKY. Uh huh. (*flipping through the pages*) I don't…I don't understand them but I think they're…I think they're beautiful.

NADYA. (*nervous, biting her nail, snatches them away*) Okay.

ROCKY. What do you mean, okay?

NADYA. I mean okay, that's all. You don't understand them, that's all.

ROCKY. What's to understand?

NADYA. Nothing. You're right.

(*After a pause, she picks up the sketchbook, closes it and leaves it on the bedstand.* **ROCKY** *walks away from the bed and stands near the chair, plays with his beer bottle.*)

ROCKY. Thank you…Thank you for showing me those.

NADYA. You can leave your money on the table. Or you can do it after.

ROCKY. Are you deliberately trying to humiliate me, or is it just some kind of afterthought?

NADYA. I said you can leave it afterwards if you want.

ROCKY. I heard what you said. I heard exactly well what you…

NADYA. Look, Jimmy. You're lonely, maybe you want romance with your fucking, or to feel we're on a date or something, but you still have to *pay*.

ROCKY. I know that. Believe me, I know that. (*pause*) Do you hate men?

NADYA. No.

ROCKY. Do you hate *me*?

NADYA. How can you say that? I just showed you my sketches.

ROCKY. But you hate this job.

NADYA. Of course.

ROCKY. Because?

(pause)

NADYA. Why do you come here? Month after month?

ROCKY. No…No you don't. *You* answer the question.

NADYA. Isn't it obvious?

ROCKY. Nothing is obvious since I met you! The more we make love, the more I obsess on you. It's supposed to be the other way around, isn't it? Isn't it the men who are supposed to be so…untouched, and the women flipping out…

NADYA. I *am* flipping out.

ROCKY. No you're not, you're just *fine*.

NADYA. I'm flipping out! In my way, I'm flipping out!

ROCKY. Not over *me*.

NADYA. Oh, that's pathetic.

ROCKY. Yeah, but true.

NADYA. What do you want from me?

ROCKY. Why did you show me your sketches? What the fuck was *that* about?

NADYA. I thought maybe you'd like them!

ROCKY. I *did*!

NADYA. So??!!!

ROCKY. It was about closeness, wasn't it? Something with no price tag! Something *human*. Here!!!…

*(**ROCKY** opens his wallet, takes a stack of bills and throws them down on the table.)*

Here's to being human!

(pause)

NADYA. Why do you come here month after month?

ROCKY. Do you want me to stop?

NADYA. No, no. I want to understand.

ROCKY. You want to understand…Let me help you understand. Okay, I keep coming back because I like you. That's a very complicated idea, but if you think on it long enough, maybe it'll sink in. Maybe I even love you. You give me no reason to, I understand. You enjoy rubbing my nose in shit. Maybe it's because I'm completely fucked up. Maybe it's just chemistry. Maybe you're just so exotic for me, but I find myself very attracted to you! As a lover. As a human being. *That's* why I come back month after month and put up with your crap. Are you happy now?

NADYA. Come to bed.

ROCKY. Now we're talking.

NADYA. How old are you?

ROCKY. Thirty-four.

NADYA. And your name's really Jimmy?

ROCKY. Why are you always testing me?

NADYA. It doesn't add up.

ROCKY. What doesn't add up?

NADYA. That you should be so alone. With your brains. With your personality.

ROCKY. Is that why you keep pushing me away? There are thousands of very smart, kind, lonely people in this city.

NADYA. Hansonia says we need a common story. A shared story, that we all have a place in.

ROCKY. What are you *talking* about? *Fuck.*

NADYA. That's when we stop being strangers. When your story has a place for me. And my story has a place for you. That's when we come together.

ROCKY. Okay.

NADYA. Simple, yes? Jimmy?

ROCKY. What?

NADYA. Come to bed.

> (**NADYA** *crawls into the bed as* **ROCKY** *undresses to his underwear, carefully folding his clothes and placing them on, or draping them over, the chair, as* **NADYA** *watches.*)

ROCKY. *(in his underwear)* I'm using the shower. Five minutes.

> (**ROCKY** *exits the stage.* **NADYA** *crawls out of bed, crosses to the chair, picks up* **ROCKY**'s *trousers and withdraws and opens his wallet. Peers at it, compartment by compartment. She puts it back into the trousers and replaces them onto the chair. She picks up a cell-phone and dials.*)

NADYA. *(into cell-phone)* Pa-ma-geé pazshalsta. Cherez pyat minoot. Da. Ho-ra-shó.

> (*She hangs up as* **ROCKY** *reenters with a towel wrapped around his waist.*)

ROCKY. You got any soap?

NADYA. Don't bother. You can go home.

ROCKY. What? What is it now?

NADYA. Rocky. Rocky with a wife and son. Or are you going to tell me that was all in the past. That you're not seeing them anymore, not since the divorce. You didn't even get visitation rights. Is that going to be the story now?

ROCKY. *(after a pause)* What did you?...Go through my wallet?

NADYA. Rocky Gonzales. There's no room for you here.

ROCKY. You know, I have a right to some privacy.

NADYA. I have a right to some *truth*!

ROCKY. No, you don't. You really don't. That's what I'm paying you for. That's the right you give up when you take my money.

> (*She picks up the bills and throws them at him. Neither of them pick up the bills from the floor where they've scattered*)

NADYA. *(calmly)* Get out.

ROCKY. Look, in a month, I'll call you.

NADYA. Don't.

ROCKY. I don't want to leave it like this.

NADYA. Go, Indian man. Work your spell on somebody else. Aren't you people supposed to be about tribe and home and family, and the truth of the spirits. How's your marriage?

ROCKY. My marriage is *fine*. Thanks for asking.

NADYA. Yes, I can see.

ROCKY. I still love you. I will always love you.

NADYA. Bla bla bla.

ROCKY. And you of course tell the truth to all your johns.

NADYA. Except for my name, yes.

ROCKY. Okay, okay…So we've reached a new level of truth. See, our stories are coming together.

NADYA. I trusted you. Sort of. So much as one can trust in this business. Kakaya dúra. Go home to your tribe.

ROCKY. I HAVE NO TRIBE! THEY TOOK IT AWAY AND MADE ME A SLAVE. WHY DO YOU THINK I'M *HERE*??!

(silence)

(From the periphery, an elegant, well-dressed and manicured woman in her late 30s named **VERA** *enters the room through the wall of light.)*

VERA. Is there a problem here?

NADYA. He was just leaving

ROCKY. Fuck you!

VERA. *(cool as ice)* Please don't talk to my staff that way.

ROCKY. Fuck you, too!

VERA. *(gathers the strewn money)* Please put your clothes on and leave.

ROCKY. *(scrambling into his clothes)* I'll shut you people down. I'll have the vice here sooner than you can blink

VERA. Of course you will.

ROCKY. Jesus, what am I saying? What am I doing?! I'm losing my mind!!!

VERA. Of course you are. We understand. Do check your wallet. Make sure everything is there.

ROCKY. *(rifling through his wallet)* Yeah! Yeah!

VERA. License?

ROCKY. Yeah.

VERA. Credit cards?

ROCKY. Yeah, fine.

VERA. Good luck to you, Mr. Gonzales.

ROCKY. Right.

VERA. Have a nice day.

*(**ROCKY** leaves, flustered. Pause. **VERA** crosses to and picks up **NADYA**'s sketchbook that she left on the bedstand. **VERA** flips through a few pages, closes the book, hands it to **NADYA**, who clutches the book of memories. **VERA** stares at **NADYA** sternly for just a moment before leaving the room. **NADYA** clutches the sketchpad, trembling.*

(Light shift to overhead spot.)

ROCKY. *(to audience)* After Vera threw me out, I found Nadya again, through her web site. Of course I changed my name. And we spoke to each other again like lovers. And there she was again, in my living room, a mirage in my son's computer, dancing for me at 2 a.m.

(Lights fade to black.)

ACT 3
("CROMWELL")

(The lights suddenly flip to a general wash as **CROMWELL** *appears.)*

HANSONIA. Detective Cromwell?

CROMWELL. Yes?

HANSONIA. Hansonia Levcourt. They told me...

CROMWELL. Yes, yes of course. Please come in, Ms. Levcourt. Have a seat.

*(***HANSONIA** *sits.)*

Can I get you some coffee, or tea, or water or something.

HANSONIA. Some water would be nice.

CROMWELL. Yes, well that we have. That we can provide. In abundance. Tapwater, I'm afraid. Is that alright?

HANSONIA. It's fine.

CROMWELL. Unless you'd care for some sherry?

HANSONIA. Water will be fine, thank you.

CROMWELL. Right.

*(***CROMWELL** *scoops up the bottle of sherry and the two styofoam cups and swiftly exits. Meanwhile,* **HANSONIA** *opens her purse and withdraws a makeup kit. Peers at herself in the mirror, pulls out an eyeline pencil and cleans a tiny blotch near her eye.* **CROMWELL** *returns with two styrofoam cups. He sets one in front of* **HANSONIA***, keeps the other for himself, remaining standing.)*

CROMWELL. You really should have tried our coffee. We have custom flavors: swamp mud, battery acid and skunk turd.

HANSONIA. Detective...

CROMWELL. Yes, I know. What are you doing here? Right. They told me you were here to post bail for Nadya. That's very good of you. I've seen kin who wouldn't do as much. I asked them to send you my way. I want you to know I have nothing against Nadya. Nothing personal.

HANSONIA. Who supervised the sting operation that led to her arrest?

CROMWELL. I did.

HANSONIA. Nothing personal?

CROMWELL. She keeps dangerous company, Ms. Levcourt. We're after her company, not her. That's why she's being released so swiftly.

HANSONIA. Are you pressing charges?

CROMWELL. Ms. Levcourt, we are the police. We stop traffic and give tickets. We give candy to small children. Then we arrest them ten years later and deprive them of their rights. But we *don't* press charges. That's up to the District Attorney?

HANSONIA. You make recommendations, no?

CROMWELL. Yes, which are often ignored.

HANSONIA. How exasperating for you.

CROMWELL. Well, yes it is, now that you mention it.

HANSONIA. Then how do you strike deals?

CROMWELL. In consultation with the District Attorney.

HANSONIA. And how close are you with the D.A.'s office?

CROMWELL. They hold us in contempt.

HANSONIA. You have their phone number?

CROMWELL. Of course.

HANSONIA. You have a phone.

CROMWELL. Oh, yes. We're very well equipped on that score.

HANSONIA. Well, then.

CROMWELL. Well then, *what*?

HANSONIA. Then you're closer than you admit.

CROMWELL. Your point being?

HANSONIA. Nadya wants to become a citizen. That will never happen if they press charges. Have them drop the charges. Please.

CROMWELL. Do you know how *expensive* a sting operation is? This is public money, Ms. Levcourt. And what do we have to show the public for its trust if we let guilty people go free?

HANSONIA. You just said you weren't after Nadya.

CROMWELL. I said we were after people far more dangerous than her. But if we don't find those dangerous people…She was prostituting herself, Ms. Levcourt.

HANSONIA. She is trying to support herself and a 10-year-old daughter.

CROMWELL. This is what employment agencies are for. Job placement centers. Trade colleges.

HANSONIA. You've obviously never watched your children go hungry.

CROMWELL. Have *you*? *(brief pause)* You are a never-married novelist, Ms. Levcourt, And a journalist with a diagnosis of clinical depression. What could you possibly know about the world?

HANSONIA. How do you know so much about my life?

CROMWELL. That's why they call me detective. But I was a composition major in college. Oooh, that was a long time ago. I have enormous respect for people like you, people who know how to command language. Commanding people is nothing, scare them and they follow, but *words*…Once I dreamed of being the next Ogden Nash. And here I am. Pathetic, isn't it.

*(***CROMWELL** *drifts off into a reverie.)*

HANSONIA. Detective?

CROMWELL. Yes.

HANSONIA. You called me here for a reason?

CROMWELL. Facts are all lies, and myths are all true. Who said that? Yeats, that's right. William Butler Yeats. Scrapping through the Irish backwoods to collect and preserve the Celtic stories. The stories, he learned, were more true than the facts they derived from. They held more meaning. A larger meaning. My job, you see, is to sort through stories, so many stories, as they rub up against each other, and my job, you see, is to credit and discredit, smooth out the edges, until we have an official story, a report, which is something like a myth, I suppose. An official truth, even more true than the facts. This is my work, Ms. Levcourt, something like Yeats', something like yours, I imagine.

(brief pause)

HANSONIA. We are adrift, sir.

(**CROMWELL** *revels in the phrasing of* **HANSONIA***'s last line*)

CROMWELL. Nicely put. *(brief pause)* You see, I hold such affection for the Irish, yet my name is Cromwell. Do you see any irony in that?

(brief pause)

HANSONIA. Not really.

CROMWELL. Everything is interconnected, of course. You are who you are because of slavery.

HANSONIA. Detective…

CROMWELL. Masters and slaves, bonded and severed by blood and economics. It's the history of the world. In America, it becomes a brutal lockstep involving everyone who sets foot on this land. Masters and slaves. You should write about *that*.

HANSONIA. I am.

CROMWELL. Good! I hope it's not more whining about abuse.

HANSONIA. It's from the point of view of a white bigot.

CROMWELL. Excellent! Something even *I* can relate to.

HANSONIA. An American creation myth.

CROMWELL. Now let's not overdo it.

HANSONIA. Detective…

CROMWELL. Yes, yes, I know. What do I want from you? Everything is interconnected. Did Nadya tell you how she came here?

HANSONIA. In handcuffs.

CROMWELL. I mean to this country?

HANSONIA. She just said she came here.

CROMWELL. In handcuffs – in a manner of speaking. I'll bet she never mentioned *that*. Indentured. It's a traditional American saga, as I'm sure you know. You're her friend?

HANSONIA. Yes.

CROMWELL. Obviously. And what is the origin of this friendship?

HANSONIA. Marc Chagal.

CROMWELL. The painter?

HANSONIA. Is there another?

CROMWELL. That's awfully highbrow.

HANSONIA. Sometimes it can't be helped.

CROMWELL. All right. So you got together to play whist with Marc Chagal playing cards that you bought at the museum?

HANSONIA. We got together so I could babysit her daughter.

CROMWELL. Katerina.

HANSONIA. Yes.

CROMWELL. In her apartment?

HANSONIA. Yes.

CROMWELL. How many times?

HANSONIA. In *her* apartment, twice. The second time, yesterday, after Nadya was arrested.

CROMWELL. And the first?

HANSONIA. Months ago, I don't know.

CROMWELL. Who answered the door?

HANSONIA. Nadya.

CROMWELL. Nobody who looked like this?

*(**CROMWELL** throws a photograph on the table. **HANSONIA** inspects it.)*

HANSONIA. No.

CROMWELL. Did you ever notice that person hanging around?

HANSONIA. Not that I remember.

CROMWELL. We think she lived in the same building.

HANSONIA. This is the person you're after?

CROMWELL. Her name is Vera. To the best of our knowledge, she is involved in – well, in addition to prostitution – all manner of schemes to raise funds. Let me count the ways: gasoline tax fraud, credit card fraud, embezzlement, extortion, racketeering and very possibly murder for hire.

HANSONIA. Ridiculous. When she could have learned some real skills at City College.

CROMWELL. My point exactly.

HANSONIA. Detective…

CROMWELL. Have you noticed strange men hanging 'round her building?

HANSONIA. I haven't been paying attention to her building.

CROMWELL. You live next door.

HANSONIA. I haven't noticed.

CROMWELL. *(throwing a number of photo on the table.)* Do you recognize any of these men?

HANSONIA. *(after perusing the photos)* No.

CROMWELL. This one's Dimitri. Dimitri Tomasian. Armenian. First, he found a way to tap into AT&T's phone lines and create his own discount long distance service. Then he set up a phony oil refinery, all on paper, to buy and sell gasoline while hijacking the taxes for his own profit. This is no fool. The F.B.I. nailed him on that one, with our help, of course. And did they thank us?

HANSONIA. Why should I care?

CROMWELL. Because being thanked is a very important courtesy! It gives one a deep-seated sense of well-being!

HANSONIA. I mean about Dimitri.

CROMWELL. You should care because you're Nadya's friend, or so you say.

HANSONIA. What's that got to do with…?

CROMWELL. I'm getting to that! You should care also because you're committed to the principle of civil rights, or so I read, under your by-line, in that petulant screed you call a newspaper. Dimitri was Vera's partner. Together, they smuggled in women from Eastern Europe, this was years ago, inviting young women to work as live-in housekeepers and such. The deal was that the women's airline tickets to America, and their housing, would be paid for by their earnings in the United States. The other part of the deal was that their passports would be held in trust. Barely speaking the language. No I.D. They slept on motel room floors and ate pasta, until somebody finally chose them to do whatever needed to be done. Their debt kept escalating according to the whims of Dimitri and Vera. Indentured servitude with a little extortion thrown in for spice. This is how Nadya entered the United States. Or so we believe. Did she mention anything of this to you?

HANSONIA. No, not a word. How do you know this?

CROMWELL. The testimony of other victims.

HANSONIA. How did Katerina get here?

CROMWELL. Nadya paid for it. How do you think?

HANSONIA. Sweet Jesus…Slavery.

CROMWELL. Sort of. Though she was calling her friends in Odessa boasting about how much money she was making here, which adds a certain nuance to her role as victim. Whatever it is, it's a cycle we're trying to break. And we will. Eventually. Perhaps you'll start to pay attention from now on.

HANSONIA. How so?

CROMWELL. Perhaps you'll go through life with your eyes a little more open. All right, never mind life, let's just start with your neighborhood. And if that's too far-reaching, how about the building next door. If you see Vera, or any of these gentlemen, perhaps you'll let me know. Here's my card. We're excellent at protecting witnesses. Believe me, we're not like those F.B.I. scum who turn in their own mothers for bonus pay. We're the Los Angeles Police Department. We have a code of honor.

(HANSONIA stares at him, jaw, dropped, not knowing whether or not he's serious. She exits. Lights dim and come up again on CROMWELL and ROCKY, at the same location.

CROMWELL. So you admit…

ROCKY. No, I don't admit…

CROMWELL. Mr. Gonzales…

ROCKY. You can't trap me…

CROMWELL. Nobody is even *trying*…You are *not* the person we're after, I don't know how much more *clear* I can…

ROCKY. How is she?

CROMWELL. She's fine! Well, no, she's not fine. She just spent the night in jail.

ROCKY. How can she?…How can you…You fuckheads, she's got a 10 year-old *daughter*!

CROMWELL. We're fully aware of…She's not the person we're after.

ROCKY. Then what was she in *jail* for?

CROMWELL. For offering a $60 blowjob to one of our undercover agents, since you asked. That is illegal, Mr. Gonzales, as I'm sure you're cognizant. Arresting prostitutes, *and* their clients, is among the many services we provide.

ROCKY. *(after brief pause)* Are you threatening me?

CROMWELL. Not really, not yet. I hadn't gotten around to that part. You're way ahead of me, Rocky.

ROCKY. You got nothing on me!

CROMWELL. We have your name and telephone number in her client book. Which is why I called you in.

ROCKY. What does that prove? Nothing!

CROMWELL. Absolutely correct. But what does it *imply*? – that's the next question. You have a wife, Mr. Gonzales? And a son? What might they *infer* from your name being in Nadya's client book? Do you know the difference between imply and infer? Did you ever go to college, Mr. Gonzales?

(pause) High school, perhaps? Did you graduate? Hit the old glass ceiling, eh? Frustrating, isn't it, I know. This isn't exactly what *I* wanted to be doing with my life. Interrogating the likes of you. Hardly my vision of a future when I was 18.

(**CROMWELL** *drifts off in a reverie.*)

ROCKY. What do you want from me?

CROMWELL. Now you're catching on.

ROCKY. The fact is…

CROMWELL. *(overlapping)* The fact is…

ROCKY. *(overlapping)* The fact is that you don't have

CROMWELL. *(overlapping)* The fact is…Mr. Gonzales.

ROCKY. *(overlapping)* You don't got shit on me. I know the law.

CROMWELL. *(overlapping)* Mr. Gonzales, be quiet.

ROCKY. *(overlapping)* You don't got…

CROMWELL. *(overlapping)* Mr. Gonzales…

ROCKY. I'm calling my lawyer, I don't gotta, what the fuck do you want with me, anyway?!

CROMWELL. Gonzales!

ROCKY. I know my rights!

CROMWELL. GONZALES! Shut the FUCK UP!

(pause)

ROCKY. *(calmly)* I know my rights.

CROMWELL. I don't believe you do. It's just you and me in a room. Do you see any witnesses? *Please* don't belittle my intelligence with blather about your rights.

(From a briefcase, **CROMWELL** *removes a gardening glove, holds it up.)*

CROMWELL. Do you know what this is?

(**CROMWELL** *lays the glove on the desk.*)

Put it on. Don't be shy.

ROCKY. Is this some kind of trap? Trying to get my prints on some...

CROMWELL. Such paranoia. Rocky, you've been watching too much Court TV. Look

(**CROMWELL** *puts it on, takes it off*)

CROMWELL. See, now my fingerprints are all over it. As they were before, I should add. Go on, try it on.

(**ROCKY** *puts the glove on, stretches his hand into its finger.*

CROMWELL. Feels good, yes? Do you know what it's made of?

ROCKY. Leather? Pigskin.

CROMWELL. Close. Actually, it's made from the scrotum of the guy before you who sat in that chair and talked about his rights.

(**ROCKY** *slowly removes the glove and sets it on the table.*)

ROCKY. That's bullshit

CROMWELL. *(smiling)* Of course it is. Honestly now. Do you really think we're such barbarians? You can't believe everything you read in the papers. Do you read the papers, Rocky? Do you?...Read?

ROCKY. Fuck you.

CROMWELL. Let me get you a diet Pepsi?

ROCKY. No thank you.

CROMWELL. I'm going to get myself a sherry. Perhaps you'll join me in a sherry?

ROCKY. No, thank you. But help yourself.

CROMWELL. All right. You're a cranky customer.

(**CROMWELL** *exits.* **ROCKY** *exhales, stares around the room. Rises from his chair. Circles the desk, paces, stops. Returns to his chair. Re-enter* **CROMWELL** *with a bottle of sherry and two styrofoam cups.*)

CROMWELL. *(grandiosely enthusiastic)* Hel-lo again!

(**CROMWELL** *sets the cups on the table, and pours a shot into each cup. Sets the bottle on the table, places one cup in front of* **ROCKY** *before picking up the other cup.*)

CROMWELL. Here we go! *(a toast)* May we be…forever young.

(They both knock back a slug.)

ROCKY. Can I bail her out?

CROMWELL. That's already been arranged.

ROCKY. By who?

CROMWELL. I'm not at liberty to say.

ROCKY. She needs to be with her daughter.

CROMWELL. She will be. Very soon. She only spent one night in our hotel.

ROCKY. And then?

CROMWELL. Then what?

ROCKY. She goes before a judge?

CROMWELL. I'm really not at liberty to…

ROCKY. Detective Cromwell.

CROMWELL. Call me Bill. Please. Like all my other good friends.

(He pours **ROCKY** *another shot of sherry. They drink.)*

ROCKY. Are you going to arrest me?

CROMWELL. For what? Infidelity and moral turpitude are still legal in this country. Thank goodness. Besides, we don't have much on you, except for your name in a hooker's address book. Which suggests, but does not prove, that you paid her a visit or two. *(placing handcuffs on the table)* No, Rocky, if I were going to arrest you, I already would pulled out these handcuffs right here, placed them on the table just like this, and said, "Mr. Gonzales, you're going down because we know you paid for nookie, in violation of penal code section 653.20 (a)." Do you have any recollection of those words crossing my lips? Do you? *(brief pause)* Rocky!

ROCKY. No.

CROMWELL. That's right. So you'll tell me nothing more than you sat in her kitchen and played gin rummy. And I'll have the good grace to believe you, if that's what you'd like. *(pause)* Is that what you'd like?

ROCKY. *(softly)* Yes.

CROMWELL. I can't hear you. My hearing's faltering as I get older. That's why I tend to shout. IS THAT WHAT YOU'D LIKE?

ROCKY. YES!

CROMWELL. Yes, *what?*

ROCKY. Yes, sir!

CROMWELL. *Please…*Call me Bill. And let's put these nasty things away.

(**CROMWELL** *returns the cuffs to his vest pocket and the glove to his case.*)

Now, when was the last time…More sherry?

ROCKY. Thanks, I'm fine.

CROMWELL. All right. When was the last time you saw Nadya?

ROCKY. In person? Seven weeks ago.

CROMWELL. How else, if not in person? *(pause)* That's a reasonable question, Rocky.

ROCKY. On the Internet.

CROMWELL. Chat room?

ROCKY. More private than that. Web cam.

CROMWELL. Why didn't you see her in person?

ROCKY. She threw me out.

CROMWELL. You beat her up or something?

ROCKY. She found out about my family.

CROMWELL. So?

ROCKY. I led her on.

CROMWELL. Led her on? That you were an eligible bachelor?

ROCKY. Exactly.

CROMWELL. Mr. Gonzales. How stupid do you think I am.

(brief pause)

ROCKY. But it's the truth.

CROMWELL. The truth is she was angling for a Green Card, and you were the chump she was setting up to marry.

ROCKY. That is not the truth.

CROMWELL. All right. Have it your way. Let's presume for the sake of argument she was smitten with you. The poor dear. The little innocent. Why didn't you tell her the truth about your family? Money was exchanged. You weren't exactly inviting her out to the high school prom?

ROCKY. To get closer.

CROMWELL. Lying is a curious way to get close to somebody. A police strategy, mainly.

ROCKY. We can each be many people. I wanted to be somebody else.

CROMWELL. You must be feeling much the same way right now, I'd imagine…So why did you pursue her?

ROCKY. Because I loved her.

CROMWELL. In my line of work, that's called stalking.

ROCKY. I still love her.

CROMWELL. *(a little embarrassed)* More sherry, Mr. Gonzales.

ROCKY. I've had enough.

CROMWELL. Evidently…Mr. Gonzales…

ROCKY. Rocky, please Bill, call me Rocky.

CROMWELL. I need to know, Rocky, why you kept pursuing her?

ROCKY. I told you.

CROMWELL. What deal went bad?

ROCKY. Love.

CROMWELL. Gonzales. If you don't stop fucking around, I'm going to pick up the phone and tell your wife absolutely everything…

ROCKY. I don't know what you want! I'm telling you the truth!

CROMWELL. I need to know, Rocky, when you called Nadya on the phone, who answered? Was it Nadya?

ROCKY. No! It was a man.

CROMWELL. And did you ever meet this person?

ROCKY. I don't believe so.

CROMWELL. You don't believe so?

(throwing a photograph onto the table)

You never saw this woman?

ROCKY. She's the one who threw me out.

CROMWELL. What's her name?

ROCKY. I don't know.

CROMWELL. It's Vera, and you know perfectly well. What was the deal that went bad? Some deal with Vera. How much money did she steal from you?

ROCKY. Steal from *me*?

CROMWELL. *(bellowing)* Look, asshole, we know you were her partner. We *know* that's why you kept after Nadya, 'cause through Nadya you could reach Vera, right? Right? RIGHT?!

ROCKY. *(plaintive, near tears)* I don't know what you're *talking* about!

CROMWELL. Then figure it out! Before I throw you in a holding cell with all the other reprobates! How does Vera operate and who does she know? Throw us a bone and all your sins are forgiven!

*(**ROCKY** collapses weeping on the table. After a pause, he collects himself.)*

ROCKY. Bill, if you can, take *me* instead, in Nadya's place. Please, just let her be with her daughter. Let her have a life here. Throw me to the wolves if you want, I don't care. I cherish her.

CROMWELL. Gonzales, Jesus...

ROCKY. Maybe she *was* guilty of what you say...

CROMWELL. *Maybe?* We've got it on fucking tape!

ROCKY. But I *know* her. She would go a straighter path if she had the chance. And a stain like this on her record can only...How is a person like Nadya supposed to make something of her life? Call my wife, tell her everything. My life is over anyway. I don't care anymore.

CROMWELL. Gonzales, what are you *saying?*

ROCKY. Call my wife. Tell her everything. Put me in shackles. What difference? I've been a slave my whole life. This is like, this is like…This is like the destiny of the Indian nations. This is like…

CROMWELL. Put a cork in it, Gonzales! How much did you drink before coming here?

ROCKY. *(indignant)* I am *not* I am *not* an alcoholic! Sorry, but that stereotype, the defeated urban tribesman. Not me. I couldn't hold a job with electric knives and saws if I was an alcoholic. But I was very nervous after I got your call and, yes, I did have a few tequilas.

CROMWELL. Which, mixed with sherry.

ROCKY. *(opening his arms, grandiose)* I am the man you see!

CROMWELL. Gonzales!

ROCKY. Please call me Rocky…

CROMWELL. Mr. Gonzales! *(brief pause as they stare at each other)*…We are clearly wasting each other's time here. Call your wife yourself, tell her whatever you want. The best would be that you'll be late, and then take a few hours to sober up. Please don't drive anywhere in that condition.

ROCKY. Okay.

CROMWELL. Thank you for your time, Mr. Gonzales.

ROCKY. Okay.

CROMWELL. You can get up now. *(pause, as **ROCKY** remains seated, frozen)*…*Can* you get up?

ROCKY. Okay

(**ROCKY** *stands with as much dignity as he can muster.*)

I'm sorry I couldn't help you more.

CROMWELL. That's all right.

(Light shift to overhead spot.)

ROCKY. *(to audience)* After Vera threw me out, I found Nadya again, through her web site. Of course I changed my name. And we spoke to each other again like lovers. And there she was again, in my living room, a mirage in my son's computer, dancing for me at 2 a.m.

*(Lights fade and come up again on Hollywood Police Station. After a brief pause, **NADYA** enters the room, standing in a periphery of light. Sensing her, **CROMWELL** faces her with a look of disdain, not lost on **NADYA**.)*

CROMWELL. This was your first arrest. Not much fun, is it. Let's hope it'll be your last. I just have a few questions and then you can be on your way. When did you first enter the United States?

NADYA. August 29, 2001.

CROMWELL. Through Los Angeles?

NADYA. Yes.

CROMWELL. So you missed seeing the Statue of Liberty? Shame. That sight proves to be an inspiration for so many of our newcomers. You entered on what kind of visa. Tourist?

NADYA. A work visa.

CROMWELL. H-1B?

NADYA. Yes.

CROMWELL. Your area of expertise being...?

(silence)

Let me guess. Computer science? You arrived on a visa that indicated you were a hardware specialist, is that correct?

NADYA. Yes.

CROMWELL. And *are* you a hardware specialist?

NADYA. No.

CROMWELL. Are you a *software* specialist?

NADYA. No.

CROMWELL. Are you any kind of specialist at all? Please don't answer that. You might incriminate yourself further...What are you going to do now?

NADYA. I don't know.

CROMWELL. Return to former habits?

NADYA. I don't know.

CROMWELL. Or try a new path? Do you know how many excellent courses they offer at City College? *(pause)* But that's not why I called you here. I need you to tell me about Vera.

NADYA. I don't know any Vera.

CROMWELL. Let me refresh your memory. *(**CROMWELL** throws a photo on the table.)* Ring any bells? Nadya, I fully appreciate your dependence on the woman. She brought you here, exploited you and helped you at the same time. It *was* she who brought you here, wasn't it? *(pause)* All right. We have to try a new game. It's called Tell the Truth. This is how it works. I ask you a question. And you tell the truth. The trick to this game is that I'm a police detective, which means that I may already know the answer to many of the questions I'm asking you. And if I know, and I know that *you* know, but you don't know that *I* know, and you stay quiet, then I know that you're not really telling the truth, and you lose points.

NADYA. They said I have the right to remain silent. They said I have the right to have my lawyer with me.

CROMWELL. Oh, Nadya, Nadya. You are absolutely correct. That's what they said and that's what they meant. But let's look at the larger picture for a moment. I ask you a few simple questions. You employ your right to remain silent. I send you on your way with a certain compassion but still perturbed by your being so stubborn. In a few weeks, right when you're in the middle of your Constitutional Law course at City College, you're going to be called before a judge to answer the charge of prostitution. It will all be a matter of public record, a record that will have been sent to the Department of Homeland Security. Now, this public record will not stand you in good stead when it comes time to renew your visa, for what, the fifth time, the deadline renewal being…? Remember, we're playing Tell the Truth.

NADYA. February 12.

CROMWELL. Correct. So by Valentine's Day, you'll realize that you're really in a bind. Your current visa expires... When?

NADYA. July 7.

CROMWELL. So you've clearly worked this out for yourself already. By the end of July you'll be egregiously out of status, your Constitutional Law course will be next to useless.

NADYA. What Constitutional Law course?

CROMWELL. You and your daughter will soon become immigrants non-status, non-gratus, you will now be forced from lack of alternatives back into prostitution, ever watching out for the LAPD and the feds, which may or may not even care, *or* which may send you to an even more unpleasant detention center at a place aptly named Terminal Island, while your daughter is placed in foster care. If you ever emerge from Terminal Island, you will be unceremoniously returned to Odessa, without Katerina, where you will do...whatever people do in Odessa. Now let's consider another option. Let's imagine this entire, unfortunate episode, the arrest, the pending charges, imagine it all just... disappearing. Poof! *(pause)* So. Let's try again. It *was* Vera who brought you here, wasn't it. It was Vera who purchased the phony visa, right? *(silence)* What was your first job here? Live-in housekeeper up on Mount Olympus? Wiping kids' snotty noses, cleaning soiled diapers, having to ask permission to walk down the hill on your so-called day off? Dodging sexual advances from the master of the house? But when he beat you, it was Vera who got you out of there. Nursed your wounds.

NADYA. So why are you asking me?

CROMWELL. To be certain.

NADYA. Nothing is certain.

CROMWELL. Nadya, in the existential evasion department, you're way out of your league. Did you or did you not work for Vera, as has been recorded in the testimony of five other witnesses.

NADYA. Yes.

CROMWELL. Thank you. That's a start. A small start. Is everything accurate I've said to this point about Vera and your connection to her?

NADYA. Yes.

CROMWELL. All right. Is she living in your building?

NADYA. Not anymore.

CROMWELL. Where is she?

NADYA. Detective Cromwell…

CROMWELL. Is she still in Los Angeles?

NADYA. I don't know.

CROMWELL. Knock it off…

NADYA. Detective…

CROMWELL. You have her phone number, I'm sure.

NADYA. She kills people, I mean she's capable…

CROMWELL. We know that.

NADYA. Then *please.*

(pause)

CROMWELL. Okay, we can get you moved to another neighborhood; another city if you want. New I.D. New life. We can do that. *(brief pause)* I'll take personal responsibility for your safety.

NADYA. Please don't make promises you can't keep.

CROMWELL. I'm a man of my word.

NADYA. I'm sure you are. You just don't understand Vera.

CROMWELL. I think I do. West Hollywood 1998. A Sheriff's deputy follows up on a truck parked illegally in a driveway. Oleg Sherell opens the door, bloodstained from head to toe, in the process of dismembering a body in the kitchen, cutting off the fingers. We were told it was Vera's work, but we were never able to pin her down. Now we have this prostitution racket, which the sting operation has made verifiable, but we're coming up a little short on some of the details.

NADYA. Please don't ask me any more questions. I've said too much already.

CROMWELL. A new start, Nadya. For you and your daughter. We know you've been trying to escape Vera's clutches for years. We know she's been threatening to hurt your parents. We can get them into the United States, to be with you and Katerina. Your whole family together again. A new start.

(pause)

NADYA. Fuck you. Fuck you and your new start. Give me one, give me one good reason why I should trust you. Because you're the *police*? In this city, there is not one, not *one* person who *ever* told me the truth, who didn't *back* out of a commitment. I'm sorry, but that is my experience. A lawyer I met. She wanted to be my friend. I said okay. I knit sweaters. She wanted a sweater for her baby. Fine, I made her one. I didn't ask anything for it. But she said she would help me with my papers. I didn't ask. She *offered*. When it's time to file my Green Card application, she's very busy, getting ready to move back to Texas. Okay, one rotten peach, you say. But this happens time after time. You think I didn't try to open a clean business here? You think I didn't try? Imported accessories from Ukraine. Hand crafted jewelry. Very simple, very classy, not folk, but trendy, things that would sell here. I took them to a shopkeeper on Franklin, we talked, we laughed, we told stories, I showed her samples. She told me what was interesting for her, what was not. She placed an order. I said let's make a contract because the rings and broaches have to be sent in from Odessa, she says, oh it's such a small order, I'm good for it, she says. I'm good for it. I spent money on that order, a few hundred dollars, no, not thousands, a small order, but that's not the point. When I call to make the delivery, my phone calls are not returned. When I show up at the shop, she's too busy to see me. What can I do? Take her to court? This is the kind of truth I find in this city, time after time. Any idiot can make it through a crisis, it's the day to day living that kills you. That's from Chekhov. Vera, only Vera kept her word. Only Vera could get me out of trouble. Where I come from, when we break our word, we know the cost. The rules are clear. And so is the cost: A broken bone. A bullet in the throat. In Ukraine we have what you people call justice. You Americans use this word, you talk about it, but you never do anything about it. Our justice is clear. Your justice is a joke. Your jails may be filled, but what's that got to do with justice? Tell me why I spent a night in jail for an honest deal struck between two adults, while that shopkeeper, who broke her word, who cost me money, sits behind her booth, counting her money and making jokes about stupid Russians. And now I'm supposed to betray Vera for *you*. For your clean life? For your new start? *Fuck* you!

(*silence*)

CROMWELL. Whenever you go for your citizenship interview, I strongly suggest you find a tone that's slightly more uplifting.

NADYA. If I broke the rules, like you people say, why are you making deals with me?

CROMWELL. I'm trying to *help* you, you stupid…

NADYA. Stupid what? Say it. Stupid whore?

CROMWELL. The woman is a killer.

NADYA. So are *you*.

CROMWELL. Madam!

NADYA. Easy to call people names isn't it.

CROMWELL. You are completely inverting…

NADYA. I know about your witness protection program. Didn't do a very god job protecting Olga Lermentova, did you? Natalia Vragova. You gave *them* your word, as well? I'm sure they took your good word all the way to the bottom of the L.A. River.

CROMWELL. That wasn't me. That was Criminal Intelligence. I'm Vice. It's a different division.

NADYA. But you must be working with Criminal Intelligence.

CROMWELL. Yes, I am. But I told you, you have my personal assurance…

NADYA. Please!…Detective…No more stories. No more lies.

CROMWELL. Fine…Fine…One moment, please.

(CROMWELL leaves the room. After a pause, KATERINA enters the room, standing in the edge of the light. KATERINA and NADYA remain at a distance from each other.)

KATERINA. Mom?

NADYA. What are you doing here?

KATERINA. Hansonia brought me.

NADYA. Oh, for God's sake…

KATERINA. Is it something bad?

NADYA. No.

KATERINA. I shouldn't be here?

NADYA. No, it's fine.

KATERINA. Where were you? Where've you been?

NADYA. Here. They needed me here very much, more than I wanted to be here.

KATERINA. Did you do something bad?

NADYA. No. They needed my help. What did you do last night?

KATERINA. Watched TV with Hansonia. Spoke with Grandma and Grandpa.

NADYA. They called?

KATERINA. No, I called them.

NADYA. Did you say I wasn't there? *(an awkward silence)* You told them, didn't you? And what did they say? Tell me the truth!

KATERINA. That I should be living with *them*.

(pause, as NADYA absorbs the blow)

NADYA. And is that what you want?

KATERINA. No! I want to be with you!

NADYA. Is Hansonia still here?

KATERINA. I think she went home already.

NADYA. And why aren't you in school?

KATERINA. I wanted to see you.

NADYA. *(after a pause)* Come here.

>   (**KATERINA** *walks over toward her mother, who embraces the child, impassioned.* **NADYA** *starts to cry.)*

KATERINA. What's wrong?

NADYA. Nothing. It's just a very difficult time, that's all.

>   *(As* **NADYA** *continues holding* **KATERINA**, **CROMWELL** *appears at the edge of the light.)*

CROMWELL. *(after a pause)* You can be on your way right after the evaluation.

NADYA. What evaluation?

CROMWELL. Family Services. They're on their way.

>   *(***NADYA** *glares at him.)*

NADYA. Family Services? What for?

CROMWELL. The judge's order, remember? To determine whether or not you're a fit mother. I wouldn't worry. I'm sure it'll be fine.

NADYA. Fit mother?

CROMWELL. The judge's order.

>   *(pause)*

NADYA. And what if I'm *not* a fit mother?

CROMWELL. In *their* view…

NADYA. In *their* view.

CROMWELL. I'd rather not think about that. And I'm sure you wouldn't either. *(Silence as* **NADYA***'s reality of losing her daughter sinks in.)* Poof. All these troubles can vanish into the air.

NADYA. A new city?

CROMWELL. Tuscon, Arizona. Fine schools. Clean streets.

NADYA. A new name. A new passport. A new driver's license. My parents rushed here, in secret.

CROMWELL. Like magic.

(NADYA is now sobbing uncontrollably, which concerns KATERINA.)

KATERINA. Mom?

NADYA. *(through her tears)* (818) 479-3294. That's her cellphone. I don't know where she lives.

CROMWELL. That doesn't matter. We'll track it through the cell. I can't thank you enough.

NADYA. Christ, what a mistake.

CROMWELL. No mistake at all. Let me take you home.

NADYA. No, that's alright we can…Of course, we have no car.

CROMWELL. Wait by the side door. I'll be there in five minutes.

(NADYA and KATERINA exit together.)

CROMWELL. *(in spotlight, to the audience/investigators)* The mistake was not her disclosing Vera's telephone number. The mistake was me driving Nadya and Katerina home. They knew Nadya had been arrested. Vera and her people, they track these events, so they were watching, they were there when Nadya and Katerina got out of the car, my car, the car of the man they came to associate with Vera's subsequent arrest, and trial, and prison term. I dropped them off at least a block away, for precisely that reason, but somebody must have noticed, because two days later, the federal marshals were ambushed.

Nadya's murder was enough for me. Too much. And so I retired. After over 40 years of service. To be truthful, they *asked* me to retire. Not because of Nadya's murder but because of some unrelated statements I made afterwards.

(To **HANSONIA***, who has entered from the periphery. The lights are now half wash, half spotlight on* **CROMWELL***.)*

CROMWELL. This is what I said: I grew up in Charleston, South Carolina. English stock, my great grandparents. The English, they say, have an affinity with the American South. The one – perhaps only – American dialect that English actors always get right is that of Dixie. Some common vowels they say, but it's really common attitudes. Aristocratic foundations. The implicit understanding that all men are *not* created equal.

I told them of how, at 14, I had run around with a lynch mob, of how I was wrongfully acquitted in the murder of an old black man, a neighborhood drunk, we hung him, for no reason in particular, decimated his body, left him dangling from an oak a mile from the highway. And they wanted me to say, these people in human resources, they wanted me to say how the experience gave me nightmares that returned over decades. But that was all nonsense, and I said so.

(He smiles.)

Yes, I'm an old bigot with blood on my hands. And if you want to understand this country, you better start with me. Stories. Everywhere stories. What is true, Ms. Levcourt, and what is trickery? Very confusing, isn't it. Perhaps together we can sort it all out. An American creation myth, you call it? The report you're writing.

HANSONIA. It's actually a novel.

CROMWELL. Yes, of course it is. Pulling together a number of stories, no doubt. Trying to have them cohere into a larger truth, like trying to create order from the motions of moths around a light.

HANSONIA. Something like that.

CROMWELL. And all told from the point of view of a white bigot, you said?

HANSONIA. Yes.

CROMWELL. From the South, of course.

HANSONIA. Of course.

CROMWELL. Perhaps the leader of a lynch mob.

HANSONIA. Exactly.

(brief pause)

CROMWELL. That was James Baldwin's idea.

HANSONIA. I know.

(pause)

And where is Katerina?

CROMWELL. They have her now. Vera's boys. We'll keep working to find her. We'll find her, you'll see.

(HANSONIA's *eyes well with tears* **CROMWELL** *extends his hand, but* **HANSONIA** *simply leaves as the light go down on* **CROMWELL.***)*

ACT 4
("VERA")

(A pool of light on **VERA**, *seated, in prison attire, addresses the audience/investigors. She holds a lit cigarette.)*

VERA. You want me to tell you that I pulled the hair of my classmates until their scalps bled? That my father and all my brothers sodomized me, and my repressed rage landed me here? Or would you like me to say I'm sorry that Nadya came to a bad end and that I had something to do with it. Alright. I'm sorry. Happy?

*(***VERA*** takes a deep hit, blows out the smoke in the direction of the audience.)*

Mind if I smoke? *(pause)* My past is none of your fucking business, and what difference does it make anyway? What's done is done. But I'll tell you a joke. An old Russian joke. Svetlana comes out of her apartment building, stepping over a pile of dog shit in the snow to get to the sidewalk; the apartment manager sees this and says, "Svetlana, is that from your dog?" Svetlana says, "Pyotr, what dog? You know I don't have a dog, but I'll clean it up anyway!" *(pause, another drag on the cigarette)* That, you see, is a portrait of my people. A nation of slaves. It was fashionable a few years ago to blame the communists for this, but you can find the trait much further back – in Dostoevsky, in Gogol, in Pushkin, they all talk about it. There's a reason we had Stalin. Did you ever have a Stalin? Twenty million people he sent to the gulag. Did you ever have anything *close*? Joseph McCarthy, and you made quick work of him. If we had Joseph McCarthy, in three months he would have been the Minister of Culture. In another three months he would have been president. *(another drag of the cigarette)* These cigarettes are shit, where'd they get these, Lithuania?

Now, may I remind you of how you took this entire country by displacing then murdering hundreds of thousands of people who were living here, fairly peacefully, before you showed up. So you know where you can shove your Bill of Rights and your equal opportunity under the law. Talk about a racket! May I also remind you of Chicago in the '20s, that your modern capitalism was pretty much jump-started by gang warfare. We're cousins, my friend. But here's the difference. You stole this country because you wanted it.

We hung on to Russia because nobody else would have it! We were there first. We didn't conquer anybody. We were just Slavs wandering around with nothing better to do.

Somebody said, okay it's either Paris or this ditch; we settled for the ditch. We didn't have your ambition, your Protestant work ethic, not even your slaves.

We had vodka, and we were *exhausted*.

When I first came to this country, I worked as a security guard at the County Museum of Art. Your monument to high culture. Minimum wage, with all the black and Armenians and Latinos and Filipino guards standing around for eight hours a day and begging for overtime. It was our job, our duty, to be invisible. And I went to some of their homes and I saw the poverty, their families, and that this was their life, all their hope, and that America also was a nation of slaves, not so different from Russia.

I am not stupid. And I quickly started to see the possibilities this country could afford, by its own standard of slavery. And that's what I did. But I was *good* to my people. I was loyal to them if they were loyal to me. Can your beloved corporations say the same?

Am I sorry? I had no choice.

And so now you're here to offer me a reduced sentence if I help you find the people who did this to Nadya... right? If they were loyal to me, I won't betray them... But they were not all so loyal. *(VERA throws her cigarette on the floor.)* I'll be out soon... *(She smiles.)* You'll see.

(Lights fade to black.)

EPILOGUE

(The bucolic piano melody from the opening movement of Schumann's "Kindersehnen" ["Of Strange Lands and People"] is heard, as the light comes up on the suspended upstage screen, and the video stream of "Betty," who, now wearing trousers and halter top, sits on the bed, staring into the camera with a Mona Lisa smile. She plays with a strap of her halter top in a motion that jerks from one frame to the next. Suddenly the image in scrambled in static, and the screen goes black.)

End of Play

From the Reviews of
BEACHWOOD DRIVE...

"...Intelligent...[a] theatrical presentation of human connection in the digital age...mines the strange dynamics of unexpected pairings...Lena Starostina is just the right mix of beautiful and faded - her stillness sets her apart: at times it reads like fierce self possession, at others like a consuming loneliness...compelling and mysterious..."
- Rachel Saltz, *The New York Times*

"...there's a sobering authenticity here, much of it provided by the first-class cast directed by Alan Mandell. [Lena] Starostina's Nadya is the center of this reality, with a conviction that never falters. [Peter] Brouwer's detective provides theatrical flavoring to the harshness, while [Brenda] Thomas' Hansonia is even able to inject a little charm into these grim events"
- Karl Levett, *Back Stage*

"Equally tender and vulgar scenes with a love-struck john, play-sessions between Nadya's daughter and a well-meaning neighbor, and a confrontation with an LAPD detective, expose the darkness of everyday exploitation. Based on a true police case, the audience is forced to consider desperation and life in modern-age slavery."
- Regina Bresler, Flavorpill.com

www.ingramcontent.com/pod-product-compliance
Lightning Source LLC
Chambersburg PA
CBHW070649300426
44111CB00013B/2344